EIGHT YEARS IN AN ORPHANAGE

Eight Years in an Orphanage

Jerry M Drumm

authorHOUSE®

AuthorHouse™
1663 Liberty Drive
Bloomington, IN 47403
www.authorhouse.com
Phone: 1-800-839-8640

First published by AuthorHouse   06/21/2011

ISBN: 978-1-4634-2703-0 (sc)
ISBN: 978-1-4634-2704-7 (ebk)

Library of Congress Control Number: 2011910621

Printed in the United States of America

This is a true story of how a young boy was raised in an orphanage. The story begins in 1956, when I was seven years old. My mom and dad were having trouble in their marriage. Mom worked one shift and Dad worked a different one. I can remember a lady babysitting me and my brother. Every day, there seemed to be an argument between mom and dad. As a little kid, you remember things that are unhappy in your life as well as the happy times. There seemed to be mostly unhappy times. Finally, after too much arguing between mom and dad, mom did not come home from work one morning. She worked the night shift in a mill. I got up that morning and found my dad sitting on the couch in tears.

I asked, "What is wrong, Daddy?"

He told me that mama hadn't come home from work. I was so young that I didn't really understand what was going on. The next thing I can remember is staying with my paternal grandmother. I can't remember where my brother was. School had started; my grandmother would get me ready for school, and my uncle would take me there.

When I was in the second grade, a lady came with my dad and my three-year-old brother to my school in Mt. Holly, North Carolina. Dad told my brother Mike and me that we would be going to another place to live. I was taken from my classroom and put into a car with my dad, a lady I didn't know, and my brother. Little did I know that my life was going to change drastically over the next eight years at Barium Springs Orphanage, which was renamed Barium Springs Home for Children in the 1950s or early '60s.

"Welcome to your new home, Jerry. I am your house parent. My name is Ms. Bartle. Come, let me show you your room and introduce you to your new roommates."

I met my new roommates, saw which bed I would be sleeping in, and was shown where to put what little clothing I had. Jacob, Tom, and Sam were my new roommates. Out of the three roomies, Sam seemed to be the friendliest. I kind of let him show me around until I could get around on my own. Remember, I was only seven years old at this point and talking about getting along on my own. My life was about to change to a degree I could never have known.

Sam took me outside, and I saw a building with a fence around the play area. The building was only about fifty yards from my new home. I saw little kids there. Sam and I walked up to the fence, and I saw my brother. He was crying so hard that I began to sob uncontrollably. Sam asked me what was wrong, and I told him that the boy was my brother. I could touch him through the fence, but I could not hug him. It felt as though if I could only reach through the fence and put my arms around him, everything would be okay. That was not going to happen. It seemed to me as though I wasn't allowed to see or play with my brother. That was the worst thing that could happen to me. At seven years of age, I felt in my heart that my brother was all alone. I went to bed that first night not knowing what the next eight years of my life would be like for me or my brother.

"Welcome to our class," said Miss Miller. My first day of school at Barium had begun. She was my second grade teacher. She introduced me to everyone in the room, about ten to twelve students. The first subject I can remember was reading. Miss Miller said we had three different levels of readers in the class. The levels were the jets, cars, and bicycles. After hearing me read, she put me into the jets class. I was a really good reader. As I began to settle into my new living experience, I became more comfortable with where I was. My main regret was that I couldn't see my brother very often. I don't think I saw him more than ten times during the entire period I was at Barium.

I met all the guys in my cottage. There were eighteen kids, ranging in age from seven to high-school age. I got along with most of the guys, but all was not a bed of roses. There were a couple of older boys who bullied some of us younger boys. One of the boys was a real bully named Larry. I was sick in the infirmary when he came to Barium. He was placed in Miss Bartle's cottage. I learned from some of the other boys that Larry was a real bully and that he had taken his brother into the bathroom and had beaten him pretty badly. You could see bruises on his brother. I stayed away from Larry as much as possible. No one ever bothered me until I was about twelve or thirteen years old. A guy in my cottage named Jesse had a bad habit of hitting people on the top of their heads with his knuckles. He had hit me numerous times before, but I hadn't done anything about it. One day, Jesse sneaked up behind me and hit me on my head with his knuckles. I turned around and hit him as hard as I could in the face. His nose started bleeding, and he ran into our cottage. I just knew he was going to tell Miss Bartle that I had bloodied his nose without provocation. To my surprise, he said nothing to her. When he came back outside, everything was fine. Jesse acted as if nothing had ever happened. From that day forward, Jesse never hit me again, and he was always very nice to me.

A new experience for me was attending church. In my short life, I had never darkened the doors of a church or a Sunday school. For kids at Barium, church was mandatory on Sunday mornings, Sunday nights, and Wednesday nights. I enjoyed going to church. It began to grow on me. Going to church was something I looked forward to. Before I could sit by myself, without my house parent, there was a man who would sit in the same seat every Sunday. He would sit in the pew right in front of me. His name was Mr. Turner, and he had to be at least seventy years old. What I remember about him was the hearing aid he wore. While the preacher was preaching, Mr. Turner's hearing aid would make a shrill sound. You could hear it all over the church. It tickled me as a young boy. Miss Bartle would always give me a stern look if I laughed about it. At age twelve, we no longer had to sit with our house parents. I began to make friends with kids who weren't in my cottage. There were about fourteen cottages on campus, each cottage with between eighteen and twenty-five people. I met a guy at church who lived in another cottage. His name was Harry. I don't know what it was, but we hit it off from the very beginning. Some Sundays, Harry and I would play a game while sitting in church. We would only start the game when the preacher started his sermon, which usually lasted about twenty minutes. We would take a piece of paper and place dots about a quarter inch apart on the paper. We would take turns drawing a line from one dot to another. The person who drew a line that completed a square would put his initials in the square. When all the lines had been connected to make squares, the person who had formed the greatest number of squares was the winner. Sometimes it would take us three or four Sundays to complete the game. After a while, Harry and I stopped playing games in church. I began to listen to what the preacher was saying. At the age of twelve or thirteen, I realized there was more to church than playing games. I was taught what the cross was all about and that Jesus died for me.

Harry was my best friend at Barium and is still a good friend of mine today. Even though he lives in New York and I live in South Carolina, we still talk at least once or twice a week. Sometimes we talk two or three times a day.

To get to the church, we had to walk about a couple hundred yards to an underpass. An underpass was a way to get to the other side of the road without having to walk across the road and risk getting hit by a car. As I got older and didn't have to walk to church with Miss Bartle, I found out that the underpass was used for other things besides walking to church. The underpass was where boys and their girlfriends would go to make out. No one could see them except the people who were either walking home, going to the gym, going to work, or using the underpass for another reason.

On Sunday morning, we attended Sunday school before going to the service in the church. Sunday school was taught in our school classrooms. One Sunday morning before the teacher came in, a kid named Billy, who was a good friend of mine, came into the classroom with a handful of pennies. He threw them into the air and yelled "grabs." All I could see were boys, me included, jumping on the floor and trying to get those pennies. Six pennies could get you a Coca Cola. Well, all the commotion caused the teacher in the room beside ours to come and see what was wrong. She saw what we were doing and reported the incident to Mr. Logan, who was supervising the boys at that time. All the boys in the class were told to meet at Mr. Logan's residence immediately after Sunday lunch. There were about ten or twelve of us in that classroom. We met at Mr. Logan's after lunch. We were all scared half to death. As we gathered in his living room, he asked Billy if anyone in the class did not take part in rolling on the floor after the pennies. Billy told him that I took no part in it. Mr. Logan gave me a tap on my rear end with the paddle and told me I could leave. I walked outside, but I could still hear what was going on inside that room. I could hear the boys yell every time they were hit with the paddle. That day was a lucky day for me. I didn't get a whipping, and I got a Coca Cola.

Mr. Logan had a funny way of dissolving disputes between boys. All kids—brothers, cousins, sisters, etc.—argue and fight with each other from time to time. Instead of giving the parties guilty of fighting a whipping or restriction, he would often have the boys put on boxing gloves and fight it out. I can only remember one time that I had to box someone. The guy's name was Luther. He was a bully and was always picking on kids who were younger than he was. He and I were at the gym, probably playing basketball or skating. I can't remember what we were doing. I do remember us getting into an argument about something. We started fighting, and immediately Mr. Logan broke it up. He told us that if we were going to fight, we were going to use boxing gloves. That was fine by me. I had never liked the little runt anyway, and I was ready to give him a beating like he had never had. We put on the gloves and started at it. Luther was about four or five inches shorter than I was. He came at me with his head down and was swinging wildly. All I did was move to one side, and then he was swinging at air. When he turned to see where I was, I hit him as hard as I could in his face. His nose started bleeding. When he saw the blood, he started crying, and Mr. Logan stopped us from fighting. I never had a problem with Luther after that day.

Our days started at seven a.m., seven days a week. During the summer months, everyone in fifth grade and up was required to work. We had our own farm, dairy, orchard, plumbing shop, carpentry shop, laundry, print shop, sewing room, and cafeteria. My first job was working on the truck farm. Mr. Houser was the truck farm boss. He was one of the best men I have ever known. We raised and picked a lot of vegetables. The rows were so long that they should have called them trips. It seemed to take forever to get to the end of a row. I remember a time we were picking tomatoes. We would put them in half-bushel baskets. When the baskets were full, we would put them onto a trailer and take them to the storage shed. After we had the trailer loaded, all of the boys, probably three or four of us, got onto the trailer. I don't remember who was driving the tractor, but when the tractor started moving, I heard a loud scream. One of the boys sitting on the trailer had the trailer tire roll over his leg. He let out a bloodcurdling scream. Mr. Houser jumped off the trailer and picked it up, with all the tomatoes on it, to free the boy's leg. I can remember Mr. Houser having back trouble after that incident.

Another job I had while working on the farm was picking up bales of straw and hay. We had to throw them onto a trailer. One boy stayed on the trailer and stacked the bales. After the trailer was full, we would have to take it to the barn and stack it. When we were hauling straw, we would try to make it fall off the trailer as we turned off the main road to go to the barn. Why we did that, I don't know. Maybe we thought we were going to get out of some work—but in reality, we had to do double work. I didn't mind hauling straw because it was light compared to hay. Hay was really heavy when it was wet.

The best job I had at the farm came as a total shock to me. I was only ten or eleven years old. Mr. Murray asked me if I had ever driven a tractor. I told him I hadn't. He told me that the present was the time to learn. I was shown where the brake and clutch were and how to change gears. He wanted me to go to one of the fields and disc it, and he asked me if I knew how to perform the task. To disc a field would be easy. I had seen it done many times. Well, I took the tractor to the field, and according to Mr. Murray, I did an excellent job. It made me feel really good to be complimented on doing a good job.

During really cold weather, we would take some of the hogs we had raised to the slaughterhouse. I don't remember very much about the process, but one trip has really stuck in my mind. It was really cold that day. There were two concrete structures that looked to me like bathtubs. I can still see one of the farm helpers shooting the hog right between the eyes. After the hog was shot, it was lifted up and placed on a big hook. One of the older farm workers took a big knife and slit the throat of the hog. After all the blood had flowed from the hog, it was then be placed in one of the tubs, which was full of scalding hot water. We rubbed the hog with some type of brush to get the hair off. After all the hair was off the hog, I think it was taken somewhere else to be cleaned, cut up, and packaged. We had country ham many times for supper.

I have another strong memory about working on the farm. I was about ten years old, and the weather was cold. We were to be at work at seven a.m. on Saturday. Well, I was there a little before seven. Some of the older boys were there also. We met in a little shack before starting work. There was a wood stove in the shack. When I arrived at work, the stove was already doing its job. It was really warm in there. Mike, one of the older boys, asked me to walk with him to the building where the hams were cured. There must have been at least a hundred hams in there. He took out a knife from his pocket and cut about five chunks of ham from five different hams. I guess he thought no one would ever notice. We walked back to the shack, and Mike put those chunks of ham on the stove and cooked them. That was some really good eating. I'm sure when the hams were cured, someone had to notice the chunks that had been cut from them.

Another memory from the farm was not so pleasant. As I stated earlier, the boys who worked on the farm met in the shack before starting work. One of the hired workers on the farm was a really big man. His name was Ben. One day as we were leaving the field to break for lunch, I stopped by the shack. Ben was in the shack. I asked him if he was going to lunch. He told me he was going to eat a sandwich he had brought with him from home. As I started to leave, I noticed what I thought was a grape soda sitting on a shelf in the shack. It looked as though no one had taken a drink from it. I asked Ben whose drink it was. He said he didn't know and for me to drink it if I wanted it. I took a swallow from it and realized it wasn't grape soda. It was kerosene or some type of heating oil. Ben knew it wasn't grape soda. He started laughing and then asked me if I had swallowed any. I told him I did swallow some. I remember him telling me that I was going to die. As I began to cry, some of the other boys were there, getting ready to leave for lunch. Ben was really scaring me, telling me I was going to die. Some of the other guys went along with what Ben was telling me.

Finally, Mr. Houser came up and Ben told him what happened. I was instructed by Mr. Houser to go to the infirmary and tell Miss Arnold what had happened. I told her what happened, and she told me that I would have to go the doctor in Troutman. I can't remember who took me to the doctor, but I can remember telling him what happened. He gave me a chalky, thick liquid to drink. I had to drink all of it, and it tasted terrible. He told me I would be okay. For all the time I worked on the farm, whenever I saw

Ben he kidded me about drinking the kerosene.

Another job I had, though I don't remember much about it, was working at the plumbing shop. Mr. Randall was the boss there. I remember he drove a 1956 or 1957 pickup truck. There were compartments on both sides of the truck to store tools and plumbing parts. Most of the time I worked there, I just stayed around the shop all day picking things up off the floor. I remember going with Mr. Randall to the cottage I lived in. There was a leak in one of the bathrooms behind the shower wall. Mr. Randall had to remove the water inlet and outlet valves to get to the leak. All I remember is standing there and watching him work. He was a very quiet man. When he had the leak fixed, we went back to the plumbing shop. I don't remember anything else about working at the plumbing shop, but I will never forget that Mr. Randall was one of the finest men I have ever met in my life. I wish all the men I knew were as nice as he was. I never worked at the carpentry shop, but the plumbing shop and carpentry shop were in the same building. I think the plumbing shop was downstairs and the carpentry shop upstairs. The boss of the carpentry shop was Mr. Everette. He was really nice to me, and I often saw him while working at the plumbing shop.

I do remember that the boys who worked at the carpenter shop were responsible for cutting all the grass on the Barium campus. There was a lot of grass to cut. I don't know if this story is true or not, but I was told that a kid named Lucas was told to cut the grass on the football field. Barium had a beautiful football field. The grass was very green. Legend has it that at one time the football field was where the hog pens used to be. Well, Lucas got on the riding mower and rode the mower to the football field. He made two full trips around the field before he realized he hadn't engaged the blade.

I have learned a great deal in my lifetime, but one of the most important things I learned at Barium was what it meant to do your very best while working, regardless of the task you were performing. All the kids, boys and girls, had a job to do when they turned ten or eleven. The girls worked in the cafeteria, laundry, sewing room, no doubt other places.

As I got older, my work ethic became stronger and stronger. After leaving the truck farm, I began working at the orchard. We had about four hundred apple trees and two hundred peach trees at Barium. The trees had to be sprayed and pruned to yield good fruit. It was hard work at the orchard. I had the feeling, even as a teenager, that I had accomplished something after a day of work at the orchard. I guess all the guys didn't have the same work ethic I had. One guy we called Spider and I had to pick up apples off the ground from under the apple trees one afternoon after school. We had to work from three p.m. to five p.m. In that two-hour period, I picked up about a dozen buckets of apples. Spider picked up one bucket of apples. He was what I called lazy. We also sold some of the peaches and apples we harvested. If you were considered a good worker by Mr. Sawyer, the orchard boss, you would get to sell the harvested fruit during its season. I was one of the kids who worked with the wife of the orchard boss selling the apples and peaches. We would sell the peaches during the summer for two dollars a bushel and the apples in the fall for two dollars a bushel. What a buy! I enjoyed picking apples, but I wasn't too keen on picking peaches. It was always hot during peach season, and I always felt itchy after getting sweaty and hot picking peaches. We also would enter apples in the county fair, which was held every fall on land owned by Barium. Our apples won blue ribbons every year. Too bad they didn't have a fair in the summer. I'm sure we would have won blue ribbons for peaches as well.

I had never seen a fair until I went to Barium. I can remember us Barium kids having red and blue ribbons pinned to our shirts. We had the ribbon pinned to our clothes so the fair workers would know we were from Barium and we wouldn't have to pay. It was so good to be able to ride all the rides at the fair. It is a wonderful memory that I will never forget.

We also had beehives at the orchard. I can remember Mr. Sawyer putting a screen-like cover over his entire head and face to protect himself from getting stung when he gathered the honey from the hives. He also had on a pair of heavy-looking gloves. We must have had at least ten beehives. I'll never forget the taste of the honey. It was so sweet. Mr. Sawyer would let us kids lick the honey that was left on the frames from the beehive after he collected it.

Barium also had its own cannery. Those of us who worked at the orchard would get to make applesauce during apple season.

The only memory I have concerning the cannery is a bad one. As I was cutting an apple, I cut the tips of two of my fingers. Mr. Sawyer couldn't get the bleeding to stop. He wrapped my fingers in a cloth and told me to go to the infirmary. The nurse, who was named Miss Arnold, took a look at my fingers. She took a roll of gauze and started wrapping it around my two cut fingers. She told me to come back in a week to see how I was doing. When I went back, she tried to pull the gauze off my fingers without unwrapping it. Well, it didn't work. In a week's time, the skin of my cut fingers had started growing over the gauze. She tried to pull off the gauze, but I wouldn't let her. It hurt really badly when she tried to do it, and I could see blood on the gauze. I had to hold my hand up. If I didn't, it would bleed. Well, after about another week, one of the other house parents saw the bloody gauze wrapped around my fingers. Her name was Miss Munday. She asked me what happened, and I told her the whole story. She told me she could get the wrapping off without hurting me. I agreed to let her help me. Slowly, she began unwrapping the gauze from my finger. As she was unwrapping it, she poured peroxide on my finger. It took her about ten or fifteen minutes to get the wrapping off. The fingers finally healed, but to this day I have a scar on both fingers, and they are still very tender.

Going to the infirmary was not something I enjoyed. I was usually pretty healthy, but one day I remember feeling really bad. Every time I took a step, my head felt as though it were going to burst. Miss Bartle told me to go to the infirmary. I went to the infirmary and told Miss Arnold how I felt. She took my temperature and found that it was over a hundred degrees. I was told I would have to stay in the infirmary until my temperature returned to normal. I believe I was there for three or four days. A vivid memory I have of my time there was the food. It was terrible. At my age, there wasn't a whole lot of food that I liked. One night for supper, I was served boiled okra. It was really slimy, and I knew I couldn't eat it, but I also couldn't leave it on my plate. Well, each room had a radiator in it for heat. I saw that the steam pipes came up through the floor. If I couldn't eat the okra, there was only one thing to do. I took the okra from my plate and pushed it through the small opening between the pipes and the floor. To this day, you couldn't pay me to eat boiled okra.

Another thing I can barely remember making is apple cider. Once a year, the Concord Presbytery would come to Barium for some type of meeting. The dining room would be full. There would be tables covered with small cups filled with apple cider. I can remember some of the men acting as if the cider were spiked. That is all I remember about that.

I became a sports fan at a very young age. At the age of five, I remember watching boxing on Friday nights with my Dad. He would let me stay up until nine p.m.

At Barium, I had the opportunity to play any sport that was in season. My favorite sport to play was baseball. I was very good at baseball and basketball. It seemed that I was always on a team with older boys. I spent a lot of time on Saturdays in the gym playing basketball. Barium High had a good football team. Going to watch Barium play football was a thrill for me. I had never been to a football game in my life. In fact, I had never seen a football game on television. About the only thing I can remember about my first football game at Barium was a player running a long touchdown. A player kicked the extra point and it was good. I can't remember whether Barium won the game or not, but I remember writing my dad a letter and telling him about the game. As I got older, I played junior varsity and then varsity basketball for my high school team at Troutman. Sports was a big part of my life, and even today I am a big sports fan.

When I started seventh grade, the Barium kids didn't have their own junior high or high school on the Barium campus anymore. We started going to a public school in Troutman, which was a mile or two south of Barium. I made friends with my new classmates. Everyone seemed to be very friendly. We weren't treated differently from the other kids just because we were from an orphanage.

The fact that I played basketball and had to practice in the afternoon didn't mean I got out of working. Boys who practiced their sports after school had to get up at 3:30 a.m. to milk the cows. When the barn was full, there were sixty cows to be milked. There were thirty cows on each side of the barn. My job was to wash the udders of the cows before the air-controlled milker was placed on the cows' udders. This was a seven-day-a-week task. Of course, the kids didn't have to work seven days a week, but the cows were milked seven days a week. I don't remember who did the weekend milking, but I know they were milked. Sometimes the cows would get out of the pasture and get into wild onions. How they could get out of a barbed-wire fence was beyond me. When that happened, it was bad news: the milk was no good. It would smell like onions and would have to be poured out.

Some of the fences we had in the pastures for the cows were electric fences. My cottage was only about a couple hundred yards away from one such pasture. When I was about nine or ten years old, one of the older boys in my cottage, Larry, whom I wasn't crazy about, asked me to walk with him somewhere. I asked him where we were going and he said not to worry about it. I walked with him down a dirt road for about a hundred yards, and then I saw a pasture. The fence surrounding it was funny-looking. It wasn't like a barbed-wire fence because there were no barbs on it. I said, "What kind of fence is that?"

He told me I was going to find out. "Touch it," he said. I grabbed the fence with my hand and got the shock of my life. The fence was electric. It scared me more than it hurt me. He tried to make me touch it again, but I wouldn't. I turned around and ran as fast as I could back to the cottage.

The dairy boss was a man named Mr. Brown. He was a big baseball fan. We would often take our baseball gloves to work and play softball if things were a little slow. Things were slow an awful lot of the time, and I remember playing a lot of ball while at the dairy. Another thing Mr. Brown had us do was rotating some of the bales of hay. If the hay was stacked only eight or ten bales high, he would have us move it out and put it on top of hay in other places in the barn. When we got to the bottom layer of hay and started moving it, mice would be everywhere. I had never seen so many mice in my life. Mr. Brown knew what was going to happen when we started moving that bottom layer of hay. When the mice started running, he started shooting. I know he emptied his pistol at least five times shooting at those mice.

We also had some tasks that we were paid for doing. One task I had was driving a tractor with a trailer to the silo on Saturdays and Sundays, filling it with silage, and taking it to the pasture for the cows to eat. I was paid seventy-five cents each day for this task. That was a lot of money back in the day to a twelve- or thirteen-year old kid. I really enjoyed working at the dairy, especially during the summertime. I only worked there for one summer, but it was a summer I will never forget.

The pastures we had seemed to be a mile long. One pasture in particular I remember was called the clover pasture. I remember it very well for one reason. During the wintertime when it snowed, this particular pasture was perfect for sledding. It seemed to me that the pasture was at least three hundred yards long. We sledded at night. I don't know where the sleds came from, but I do remember them being there. The pasture had about three terraces in it. The end of the pasture leveled out, and there was a creek at the very end of it. When we sledded, it was all we could do to get the sled turned to keep from going into the creek. I can remember someone bringing wax shoe polish to the pasture. It had to be one of the older boys. They would strike a match and light the shoe polish, which they had placed along the sledding route. It helped us see where we were going at night. It seemed as though the shoe polish would burn forever. One time when the snow had begun to melt, we had to move to another pasture that had more snow in it to sled. We didn't have any shoe polish to help us see where we were going. I remember going down the hill, and before I knew it, I was in the creek. My toboggan had slipped over my head, it was dark, and I thought I was going to drown. I got the toboggan off my head, got out from the creek, and headed to my cottage, which was about half a mile away. When I got home, my clothes were nothing but a sheet of ice. Miss Bartle asked me what happened, and I told her I fell into the creek. I got my frozen clothes off and put on my pajamas, but I was still cold. I can remember her wrapping me up in a blanket to get me warm.

There was an eighth-grade teacher whose name was Mr. Landis. He was a big man, six feet six inches tall, and was also an ex-marine. He would always ask how we were treated by the house parents at Barium. Someone must have told him not very well. Mr. Landis said if he were at Barium, he would make things better. Well, he got a job at Barium and was over all the boys. He was not my favorite person. He was very strict and demanding. I'm sure this was the marine coming out. As I was going to the silo one Saturday to get silage to feed the cows, I decided I would drive down the highway about half a mile and get myself a pack of cigarettes. I bought my cigarettes and started back up the road. As I turned to head to the silo, I saw Mr. Landis in his car heading toward me. Only by my quick thinking was I spared being restricted or whipped with a paddle. I placed my cigarettes in a secret compartment under the seat of the tractor. Mr. Landis asked me where I had been. My reply was that I went to the store to get a Coca Cola. He asked me where the Coke was, and I told him that I drank it at the store to avoid paying a two-cent deposit on the bottle. Well, he didn't believe me. He accused me of going to get cigarettes. I had to get off the tractor and let him frisk me. Of course, he didn't find my cigarettes at this time. I went about my job of going to feed the cows. A few days later, Mr. Landis went to my cottage, searched my closet, and found the cigarettes. There was only about a half pack left. He confronted me and told me he had found the cigarettes. My punishment was restriction for one week. I could only go to work and to church. What a bummer, having to stay in my room while not at work or church. I couldn't watch TV, but I could listen to the radio I had in my room. That was one of the longest weeks of my life.

I really enjoyed going to Troutman School. I was able to meet new friends. It was always good to get away from Barium for a while. When we started going to high school, we were allowed to go to Statesville on Friday and Saturday nights. Barium had its own bus, and one of the older guys would drive it. My best friend Harry and I would usually go to the pool room or to the movie theater. One Friday night, I walked over to Harry's cottage because the bus picked us up in that area for the ride to Statesville. I remember wearing a brown button-up sweater with pockets on each side of it. I had two cigarettes in my sweater pocket. As I walked into Harry's cottage, I saw Mr. Landis right behind me. I still to this day can't figure out how a man that big could sneak up on me that fast. He asked me where I was going, and I told him that Harry and I were waiting to catch the bus to Statesville. As usual, he frisked me and found the two cigarettes.

He said we had a choice. We could take a beating, which would be three hits on the rear end with a radiator brush, or be restricted for a month. Harry didn't even smoke; he got into trouble just because he was with me. Well, we decided to take a beating instead of being restricted for a month. Mr. Landis asked who wanted to be first. What a stupid question, I thought. I said I would. Mr. Landis told me to put my hands on the wall and stick my rear end out. I did as he said. He hit me so hard with that radiator brush that I felt as though I was going to pass out. I had to wait for at least a minute before I would bend over to be hit again. Well, I took my three licks, rubbing my rear between licks. Then it was Harry's turn. He put his hands on the wall, and Mr. Landis hit him really hard. Harry didn't even flinch. He was hit a second time, and the radiator brush broke in half. In case you don't know, the wood on a radiator brush is about a quarter-inch or a half-inch thick. Mr. Landis told us to go on to Statesville.

I was caught smoking another time by Mr. Landis. As I was walking back to the orchard after lunch one day, I took a shortcut down a hill next to Genny Gilmer cottage. The shortcut would take me through a small patch of woods. I stopped in the woods to smoke my cigarette. After

I finished smoking, I proceeded on through the woods to the orchard. Mr. Landis was waiting for me as I exited the woods. He asked me if I had been smoking, and naturally I told him no. He grabbed my hand and smelled the fingers on my right hand. He could smell the cigarette smoke on my fingers. Of course, I told him I hadn't been smoking, but that didn't matter to Mr. Landis. He told me to go on to work and said he would deal with me later. Well, later came the next Saturday. We had a pond at the back of some of the farm property that we fished in. Around the pond were brush, small trees, and weeds. Mr. Landis took me over there on Saturday after lunch.

He handed me a bush ax and told me he wanted all the small trees cut down. I was told I had two Saturday afternoons to get the work done. The first Saturday, I worked my tail off cutting down small trees. Mr. Landis came to check on me close to five p.m. He could see that I had really been working. I was very tired and hungry, and he told me to get into the car. Mr. Landis took me home and said that he would come and get me the following Saturday to finish my punishment. I was really dreading that following Saturday. True to his word, he took me back to the pond to continue cutting down trees the next week. There must have been hundreds of trees around that pond, or so it seemed. Well, I cut trees down with the bush ax until he came back at five p.m. He asked me if I was tired, and I said I was. "Are you ready to go home?" he asked.

I told him I was and said I was glad I didn't have to come back to cut more trees down. Mr. Landis told me the area around the pond looked good and that I had done a good job. Then he told me to enjoy my walk home. He took off in that ugly brown station wagon he drove. I started walking home, which was about a mile or mile and half from where I was. I was dead tired when I got home.

There was a guy named Archie in my sophomore class who had a driver's license. We struck up a casual conversation one day. As we were talking, he asked me how I liked it at Barium. My reply was that it wasn't so bad. I had been at Barium for eight years, had good friends, and had really settled in very well.

"Do you ever go to Statesville?" Archie asked

"We can go on Friday nights during the summer months," I replied.

Archie asked if I had ever drunk beer.

"Are you kidding me?" I replied.

"No, I'm not kidding. Plenty of the Troutman boys drink beer," he said.

What a shock that was for me. Archie asked if I would like to go with him to Statesville and get a few beers some night.

"Sure, why not," I said.

We decided Archie would pick me up at nine thirty the following Friday night. I had already told him what cottage I lived in. He had gone by earlier to check it out. My cottage was perfect for sneaking out at night. It faced the woods, and my room was on the side that faced the woods. A dirt road in front of the cottage ran to Highway 21. Well, Friday night rolled around. A little before nine o'clock, I went to my room and waited for Archie to come pick me up. Just like clockwork, Archie arrived. I slowly raised the window, climbed out, lowered the window, and ran to Archie's car. This night, I was going to experience something I could have never imagined. The ride to Statesville took only five to ten minutes. Archie knew exactly where to go to buy beer. I guess things were different back in the day as far as having an ID checked. He bought a six-pack of country club malt liquor. I remember the cans being really small. Archie opened a can and handed it to me. That first taste I will never forget. It was *terrible*. How in the world could someone drink something that tasted that bad?

"Archie, are you telling me beer is supposed to taste this bad?"

"No, you will develop a taste for it the more you drink," he replied.

Well, I finally got that first beer down somehow. The taste was terrible, but I started drinking another one. After riding around Statesville for about thirty minutes and sipping on my second beer, I told Archie something was wrong with my eyes. He just laughed and told me I was getting a buzz. I had no idea what he was talking about when he mentioned a buzz.

"What is a buzz?" I asked.

"A buzz is when you are starting to get drunk. Do you feel okay?" he asked.

"I think I'll be okay." I finished the second beer and was feeling no pain. We had been riding around Statesville for about an hour. I started on my third beer. What a mistake. Everything started spinning around and around. I can remember Archie really laughing. He must have been through this before.

"I need to go home, Archie."

"Are you sure?" he asked.

"I'm really sure," I replied.

The next thing I remember is Archie stopping the car at my cottage. Somehow, I managed to get to the window, climb in, get my clothes off, and get into bed. I don't know what time it was, but I was feeling sick. I was so drunk that I couldn't get out of bed and make it to the bathroom. I began to get sick and could do nothing but hang my head over the bed and start throwing up. Sam, who was in the bed next to me, asked what was wrong with me. I told him I was sick. He knew that I had gone to Statesville with Archie.

"I drank too much beer, Sam, and I'm getting sick." I began throwing up on the floor between Sam's bed and mine. I don't know how long I threw up, but I know Sam stayed up with me until I passed out. Sam had gotten towels and cleaned up the puke from the floor. When wake-up call came at seven a.m., the house parent, Miss Bartle, opened the door. I can't imagine what she thought. The smell had to be horrible. Sam told her that I had gotten sick during the night. I can't remember what she said, but I do remember cleaning the mess up with Sam's help. What a true friend. I felt bad all that day. It was Saturday, and I didn't have to work. I don't think I could have worked if I had to that day. Later that day, in the afternoon, I walked over to my girlfriend Sallie's cottage. She told me I didn't look too good. I proceeded to tell her what had happened. I can't remember her response, but I do know my drinking days were over.

Sallie was the first girl that I really cared about. She was my first girlfriend and the first girl I ever kissed. I was in love for the first time in my life. I mainly spent time with her when I walked her home from supper. At times, I would walk over to her cottage, which was next to mine. We would sit around and talk. I have no clue what we talked about, but I felt good when I was with her.

There was a time when a man named Mr. Logan was supervising the boys at Barium. He was a chain-smoking, short fat man. During the summer months, it wasn't unusual for boys, and possibly girls also, to sneak out of the cottage after lights were out. My best friend Harry and I sneaked out at least three or four times a month. We would just walk around the campus figuring out what we could do. I can remember us breaking into the cafeteria kitchen. We found where the popsicles were kept and proceeded to eat them until we couldn't eat anymore. I think we sneaked out at night just to see if we could do it without getting caught. We were caught sneaking out only a few times. The first time we were caught was really interesting. Harry and I found a way to break into the kitchen. Mr. Logan caught us as we were coming out of the cafeteria kitchen. He asked us what we were doing, and we told him the truth. He asked us how many times we had sneaked out at night. I replied that we had done it fifteen or twenty times. You could have blown him over with a feather when I told him that. He must have thought we had only done it a few times. He restricted us to our rooms for one week for that episode.

There was another time when a friend of mine, whom we called Grunt, sneaked out with me. We were just casually walking around the campus, not getting into any kind of trouble. We were just out for the thrill of doing something we knew we weren't supposed to do. There was no rhyme or reason to why we were out, except that we knew we could smoke when we sneaked out. We figured there was a low chance of us getting caught. Well, surprise, surprise. Grunt and I were walking on the lower side of the campus, next to the boiler room. An old garage was next to the boiler room. I told Grunt, "Let's take a smoke here."

We stepped behind the garage and lit up. Out of nowhere, Mr. Logan appeared. We were caught again. Our punishment this time was two licks with a paddle. It was nothing like what Mr. Landis had done to me when he caught me with cigarettes in my sweater pocket.

My time at Barium was not just a time of getting into trouble by doing childish things like sneaking out at night or smoking when I knew it was against the rules. We had a swimming pool, a softball field, a gym, and a football field on campus. The gym was where we would go on Friday and Saturday nights when we were in grades five through twelve. Of course, most of the high-school boys went to Statesville on Friday and Saturday nights. We skated in the gym. I never had been on a pair of skates in my life until I came to Barium. It took me quite a while to get the hang of skating. Some of the older boys and girls could skate really well. The gym was also used for dancing. I remember girls dancing with girls. There were not too many guys dancing. I was so shy and backward at that time that there was no way to get me onto that gym floor. I had no clue how to dance. My thought was that a gym was used for playing basketball. Playing basketball was what I enjoyed, and I spent many hours playing the game.

Barium also had a swimming pool. The pool at Barium was the first one I had ever seen that was built into the ground. I didn't know how to swim when I went to Barium, but I learned very quickly. One of the older boys threw me in water over my head. It was either sink or swim. I can remember one of the older boys pulling me out of the deep water. I probably would have drowned if he hadn't gotten me into shallow water. I had been at Barium for about three or four years when a new pool was installed. It was really nice. There were diving boards, which I was able to use because I could swim really well by then. I knew I could swim out of the deep water to the ladder without any problem. Summertime was always fun at the pool. At times, we would have watermelon to eat after swimming at the pool. They were grown on the Barium farm. I always looked forward to the watermelon feasts.

The annual shrine bowl football game was an annual event held at Memorial Stadium in Charlotte, North Carolina. It was a game played between the best high-school players from North Carolina and South Carolina. The Barium kids would get to go to the game every year. I can't remember how many times I went, but I remember one time really well. We always rode the Barium bus to the game. The bus was the first flat-nosed bus I had ever seen. When we would get into the Charlotte city limits, a Mecklenburg county policeman would give us a police escort to the stadium. Our seats were always on the fifty-yard line. We had all we wanted to eat, and I took advantage of it. I don't know how many pecan rolls I ate, but I do know there were enough to make me sick. I spent part of the game in the bathroom throwing up. I don't have a clue who won the game, but I do know I didn't eat another pecan roll for many years.

Christmastime was the best time of the year, especially when I was seven to ten years old. Fred Kirby, the eternal cowboy, would come to Barium. All the kids would gather in the gym. Mr. Baker, the superintendent at Barium, and Fred Kirby would have a shootout. As a kid, I thought the bullets were real. When the guns were shot, the sound was deafening. Mr. Baker seemed to win the shootout every year. Before we left the gym, all the kids were given a sack containing nuts, candy, oranges, and I don't know what else. I do know the sack was full, and it seemed to last for weeks.

We also wrote letters to Santa. I can remember asking Santa for a radio one Christmas, and I got it. All the presents for the kids in my cottage were placed in one of the empty rooms in the cottage. We could stand on a block of wood outside the window and look into the room. The first time I looked in that room, it looked as though there were at least a hundred presents there. You know how a young kid sees things, especially when he had never seen anything like that before.

Another good memory at Christmastime is of attending church. I was taught at Barium the true meaning of Christmas. Christmas Day was Jesus's birthday. That is what Christmas is all about. That is the most important thing I learned while at Barium. We also got to go to Davidson College during the Christmas holidays. The Davidson students were really nice to the kids. While there, we would also get more fruit and candy. Some of the Davidson students would come to Barium on Sunday mornings and teach Sunday School. My teacher when I was in the sixth or seventh grade was Jim Haney. He played basketball for Davidson. Some of the Davidson students would also come to Barium on Saturdays during the summer and play softball with the kids. All of them were very nice to the kids. Even today, I and a friend of mine go see Davidson play basketball. I even saw Jim Haney at a game one night. I talked to him and let him know that I was at Barium in the sixties and that I appreciated all he did for the kids there.

Mealtime was a big deal for me at Barium. It seemed to me that I was always hungry. One thing I can say for the kids who were at Barium is that we always had plenty to eat. We had a big cafeteria to eat in. I don't know how many people it would seat at one seating, but as a young kid it seemed like hundreds. My earliest memory of eating a meal in the cafeteria was when I was seven years old. I had been at Barium for only a couple of days. Breakfast was being served. We had fried eggs. I can't remember if we had grits or anything else with them. What I do remember is telling the house parent I couldn't eat an egg with the yellow in it. I found out later that an egg cooked that way was "sunny side up". My house parent, and it wasn't Miss Bartle, told me that I had to eat it. I tried to explain to her that

I couldn't. I told her it would make me sick. She didn't know what was going to happen if she made me eat that egg. Well, I was forced to eat it. I didn't eat but one bite of it. As my teeth bit into the runny yellow part of the egg, I put my hand over my mouth. The runny part of the egg started running through my fingers. I was getting sick as the egg started coming out of my mouth. As best as I can remember, I was never forced to eat another egg sunny side up.

Some meals we had at Barium were very good. My favorite, which we got about once a month, was barbecue. There were eight people to a table. The house parent sat at the head of the table. There were three people on each side and one person at the end of the table. My place at the table was the first seat to the left of the house parent. The food always was passed to the left, which meant I was the first kid to get his food. When barbecue was served, I would have one sandwich eaten before the bowl was passed all the way around the table. We could eat as much as whatever was served as we wanted, until the food was all eaten. I can remember eating five barbecue sandwiches at one setting. Even today, I am always the first one finished eating with whomever and whatever I eat.

After we were dismissed from the dining hall, I would run as fast as I could to my cottage. The cottage faced the woods, so I would go to that side of the cottage and smoke a cigarette. It only took me about two minutes to finish a cigarette when I had to hurry. I would wash my hands with soap and water to get the cigarette smell off my fingers. A tube of toothpaste was always handy to put a little into my mouth and hold it there for a while to get rid of the smoke smell. I bet Miss Bartle wondered why my teeth weren't shiny and white if I was using that much toothpaste.

Speaking of toothpaste, I remember the first time I went to the dentist at Barium. My teeth were in terrible shape. I was told that the dentist came to Barium once a week to work on the kids' teeth. The first time I visited him, he told me that my teeth weren't the worst he had seen, but they could be a lot better. Dr. Lansing, the dentist, was a very nice man. It seemed to me as if I were going to the dentist every week for a long time. When I was about thirteen years old, Dr. Lansing had to put braces on my teeth. I had braces on for about two years. If I remember correctly, when we had to have a tooth drilled, there was no numbing procedure. He just started drilling. He would drill, baby, drill. I still to this day don't like going to the dentist. But the dentist was a very nice man. One thing I did back in the winter of 2010, was talk to Dr. Lansing. I got his phone number from a friend of mine and gave him a call. He remembered me and was glad I called. He and his family are doing very well. He is eighty-two years old now.

A lot of people on the outside looking in thought Barium was a perfect place. They seemed to think we had it made. I'm sure we had it better than some kids, as far as having our physical needs met. We had clothes to wear, food to eat, and a bed to sleep in. However, everything wasn't a bed of roses. In the summertime, we would get to play outside until nine p.m. I remember one night when Miss Bartle called us in at about nine. We, as most kids do, didn't come in on the first call. All but Enos came in shortly after nine. Miss Bartle called Enos again, and he still didn't come in. He was talking to a girl who lived in the cottage next to ours. After about fifteen minutes, Enos came in the door, and Miss Bartle met him. I remember her grabbing his ear and pulling him into the house. Enos turned and hit her with his fist and broke her glasses. That was the wrong thing to do. I knew as soon as he hit her that he was in big trouble. Hitting a house parent was like shooting the president of the United States. Mr. Baker, who was the superintendent at the time, was called to our cottage. After he arrived, Miss Bartle told him what had happened. He told me to go outside and get him a hickory. I did as he said. When I came back inside, I handed him the hickory. He said to me, "Boy, I said get me a hickory, not a twig."

He sent another boy outside to get one. When the boy came back in, he had a small tree in his hand. It was about as big around as your little finger. Mr. Baker made all the kids in the cottage watch as he beat Enos with what he called a hickory. He beat him from the top of his back to his ankles. I can remember looking at Enos's back the next day. He had welts all over his back and legs. If I had ever thought about hitting my house parent, that thought was gone from my mind when I saw what happened to Enos.

Another story I remember involving Enos and me was not a very pleasant one. Our cottage was next to the baby cottage. There was a huge fig tree behind the baby cottage. Next to the fig tree there were some steps, about five or six, that led to the basement of the baby cottage. Enos walked down the steps, but couldn't get in the door because it was stuck. After he pushed and pushed on the door, it opened. We both walked into the basement but didn't see much in there. I remember seeing some old chairs stacked up there. As we looked around, Enos saw another door on the other side of the room. He peeped through the door and decided he wanted to go in there. The door was locked, so he looked around on the floor to see if there was something that would help him get into that room. Finally, Enos saw a nail on the floor that looked as though it was a foot long. He picked the nail up, and I asked him what he was going to do. He said he was going to break into that room. There was a light switch on the wall. He took the cover off, and what happened next scared me as badly as anything in my life to that point. Enos got the cover off the light switch by beating on it with a steel bar that was lying on the floor. We could see a bunch of wires in there. He took the big nail and jammed it into all those wires. Enos began screaming and couldn't let go of the nail. I kicked him, and the nail fell from his hand. He and I ran up the steps as fast as we could. Enos sat down on the grass and started rubbing his legs. He told me his legs felt as though they were on fire. I felt fine but was really scared. One of the boys playing outside saw Enos and me as we came up the steps. He saw him sitting on the ground rubbing his legs and knew something was wrong. The boy ran into the house and told Miss Bartle that something was wrong with Enos. She came out to see what was going on. We told her what had happened, and she told us to go inside. I think she called Mr. Logan, but I am not sure. All I can remember is that Enos and I were restricted to the cottage for a week. I later found out that Mr. Logan told Miss Bartle that Enos was lucky to be alive after what he did. Enos could have been electrocuted. He was standing in some water when he jammed that nail into the wires inside the light switch. Those wires were live wires. As kids we do stupid things sometimes. That was something that neither Enos or me should have done, but we did learn that electricity can bite you.

I always loved the summertime better than cold weather. As boys, in the summer we were always doing something, whether it was playing ball, swimming, playing hide and seek, playing tag, or doing anything active. We didn't have to work on Saturdays in the summertime. My best friend Harry and I, and one or two more boys whose names I can't remember, decided we would walk through the woods to Mr. Luck's pond. It was only about a fifteen-minute walk through the woods. You had to be careful getting down to the edge of the pond because the hill leading down to it was very steep. We would hold on to tree limbs as we worked our way slowly to the edge of the pond. During the summertime, you could get within ten feet of the water, and no one on the other side of the pond could see you because of the thick foliage. That day when we got to the pond, a small wooden boat was tied up right at the place we were. The boat must have been about ten to twelve feet long. It had a paddle in it and we didn't see any water in the boat, so we figured in wasn't leaking. Well, one of the boys decided he was going to get in the boat and paddle around the pond for a while. Harry and I said we would just watch. The other boy wanted to get in the boat also. He got into the boat, and after he sat down, I pushed the boat away from the bank. Well, surprise—the paddle was not in the boat. It was lying on the bank. They must have been about ten to fifteen yards from the bank when we heard a man screaming at the top of his lungs. Harry and I could see him, but we were sure he couldn't see us. It was Mr. Luck. He yelled for those boys to get back to shore and get out of the boat. They told him they didn't have a paddle. Mr. Luck continued walking toward the pond. As he got closer, we heard him say to the boys in the boat, "Tell your buddies I see them standing in the woods and they are in trouble also."

When he said that, Harry and I hightailed it up the bank and ran all the way home. To this day, I don't know what happened to those other two boys who were with us. I do know that we didn't stop sneaking down to Mr. Luck's pond. We went down there pretty often during the summertime, and at times we would swim there, even though we had a very nice swimming pool on the campus. Other times, we would fish or just sit and look at the water and talk about what we would be doing if we weren't at Barium. Mr. Luck's pond was a place that seemed as though it was a thousand miles away from Barium, and yet we were only about a mile from going back to reality.

At times, some of the kids would go down to a little store named Dottie's. It was only about half a mile down Highway 21. Of course, we couldn't walk down the highway. We would go through the woods and end up directly behind the store. This is where we would buy our cigarettes. Dottie knew we were from Barium Springs, but she would always sell us cigarettes. I remember being in Dottie's store one day when another

Barium boy came in. His name was Roger, and he was older than I was. He and Dottie seemed to know each other very well, judging by the way they talked to each other. There was a gum ball machine in the store. It cost one penny to get a gum ball from the machine. Some of the gum balls were speckled, and the others were a solid color. It looked as though it was one fourth to half full. I saw Roger pick the gum ball machine up, turn it upside down, and start shaking it. When he got a speckled gum ball positioned so that it would be the next gum ball to come out of the machine, he would slowly turn the machine over and place a penny in it. Out would come a speckled gum ball. Speckled gum balls were worth a nickel. Roger would do this five times. When he got his five speckled gum balls, he would buy a pack of cigarettes. It seemed as though Barium kids were prepared for every situation that would arise. What other kids would do what Roger did? Instead of paying a quarter for cigarettes, he paid a nickel. At the time, I thought it was really cool, but now I know what he did was dishonest. It was also dishonest for me to sit and watch him do what he did, thinking that it was okay for him to do it and me not to tell him that what he was doing was dishonest.

Everyone has to remember summer vacation. That was when most of the kids went back to their families for two weeks. It was very nice to go back to Mt. Holly, North Carolina, and be reunited with my grandmother, cousins, aunts, and uncles. My dad was living in Flint, Michigan, and he would drive down for the two weeks my brother and I were home. We stayed with our grandmother. Grandma would fix us anything we wanted to eat. My favorite, and I don't remember getting it at Barium, was fried chicken. It was so good. She also made all kinds of pies and cakes. Not being partial or anything, but she was the best cook I have ever known. The two weeks we were away from Barium went by really fast. It was a time I could reunite with my brother, whom I didn't see much at all while at Barium. In no time, we were back in the same routine we had left only two weeks prior. Some of the kids didn't get to leave for a two-week vacation. I don't know if they didn't have any family to go to or if they just wanted to stay at Barium and work. I was told by some of the guys that when they worked during vacation time, they were paid. I'm thankful that I had family to visit, and I have a special place in my heart for those who didn't. Speaking of family, most of us have brothers, sisters, cousins, and so on. But after spending eight years at Barium Springs, I found out that my true brothers and sisters are the ones I spent time with at Barium. There is a bond there that can never be broken. I am thankful to God for each and every one of them who has crossed my path in some way.

When I was about eight years old, Mama came to Barium to see my brother and me. I don't remember much about that visit, but I knew that she was my mama, that she loved me, and that I would see her again someday. I was never told what happened to my mama until I was a teenager. I had heard many lies about what happened, and I didn't understand why a mother would do what I was told she did. My dad told me she didn't love me or my brother. I carried that weight with me until I was twenty-two years old. I decided I wanted to see my mom one day. I called her. Mama came to see me the next day, and I found out the truth about what had happened between my mama and my dad. Mama and I have been really close since that day.

In 1963 or 1964, Miss Bartle retired, and Miss Jones became our new house parent. We didn't get off on the right foot from the very beginning. There was something about this lady I didn't like, and I'm sure the feeling was mutual. It seemed as though I was doing something to get under her skin all the time. I remember being restricted to my room more times than not. I really wasn't a bad kid. She had a problem, and I don't know what it was. She seemed to be taking it out on me. All I did was go to school, work, church, and to the ball field or the gym on Saturdays. It got to the point that I didn't want to go to my cottage. I really missed Miss Bartle. After Miss Jones had been my house parent for about a couple months, she caught me smoking. The only good thing I can say about getting caught is that I didn't get a beating from Mr. Landis. Miss Jones restricted me to my room for one month. I couldn't go outside and shoot basketball, which was something I loved to do. The only places I was allowed to go were work and church. I couldn't even go to the TV room. I felt like a prisoner, and I'm sure Miss Jones was thrilled. From that point on, I hardly spoke to the lady (I use the word lady loosely). If she asked me something, I would answer her, and that was all. I probably didn't say ten words to her the rest of the time I was at Barium.

School was out for summer vacation, and I was going to be a junior in high school come fall. I was what was considered a "big boy" now.

I think all junior and seniors were considered "big boys." Things were going just fine. Sallie and I were getting along really well. Harry and I were going to Statesville most Friday and Saturday nights. Things couldn't have been better, or so I thought.

One day after supper, I made my usual run to the cottage to take a smoke. Well, I got caught by Miss Jones. She must have run to the cottage to catch me smoking; usually, she stopped and talked to some of the other house parents. By then, I knew the drill. I was restricted to my room for one month. I could do nothing but go to work and church. Not getting to talk to Sallie is what really bothered me. Well, things were about to change. A couple days earlier, I had received a letter from my Dad. There was a twenty-dollar bill in the letter. Twenty bucks was a lot of money back in the day. It didn't take me long to figure out what I was going to do. I was going to run away from Barium and go to my grandma's house in Mt. Holly.

It was a Friday night. Lights had to be out at nine. I guess it was about ten or ten thirty. The time was now. My bed was right next to the window, and my cottage faced the woods. I slowly raised the window and was ready to go out. Before I could get out the window, Jacob asked, "Where are you going?"

I told him I was running away. He asked if he could go with me. I told him to come on. Well, we both got out the window. All we had were the clothes on our backs and a twenty-dollar bill. We ran up to Highway 21, which was only about a hundred yards from our cottage. We were going to thumb a ride to the bus station in Statesville, which was about five miles from Barium. The first car that came by stopped and picked us up. I can remember to this day that it was a 1964 Chevy Malibu. The man asked where we were going, and I told him to the bus station in Statesville. When we arrived at the bus station, I went to the ticket window and bought two tickets to Charlotte, North Carolina. Jacob and I tried to sleep on the way to Charlotte, but to no avail. The ride must have taken about an hour. We finally arrived at the Charlotte bus station. As soon as we got off the bus, I saw a yellow cab sitting across the road from the bus station. Jacob and I walked over to the cab. The driver was asleep. I tapped on his window, and he looked up. I asked him if he could take us to Mt. Holly and what would it cost. Mt. Holly was about fifteen miles away. The driver told me he would charge eight dollars. We jumped in and were on our way to my grandma's house. When I left Barium, I had twenty dollars in my pocket, and I was still going to have five bucks left when I got to Mt. Holly. We arrived at Grandma's house at one a.m. She had a screened-in back porch. In the summertime, she would lock the screen door by placing a latch on the door into a hook next to the door. I'm sure most of you older folks know what I am talking about. She would leave the main door open so some nighttime air could come into the house. Well, for some reason the screen door wasn't latched that night. Jacob and I walked into the kitchen, and in no time, grandma was facing both of us. Her words were, "Jerry, you have run away."

I said yes and introduced her to Jacob. She had an extra bedroom, which I took. Jacob slept on the fold-out couch. The next morning at eight, Miss Sisk was there to take us back to Barium. I told her I wasn't going back, but Jacob had to go back. He was only fourteen years old. I was fifteen but would turn sixteen in September. Miss Sisk asked me what I would do about the braces on my teeth. My reply to her was I would get them off. Miss Sisk left with Jacob, and my Grandma called my Dad, who was living in Michigan. She told him the whole story. Dad said that if I wasn't staying at Barium, neither was my brother Mike. We went the following Tuesday and picked up Mike. Mike lived with our uncle until he graduated from high school.

My dad came home from Michigan for his annual summer vacation about a month after I had run away. He asked me about the braces on my teeth. I knew that Dr. Lansing, the Barium dentist, had his office in Salisbury. My dad called him, and we went to see him the next day. Dr. Lansing told us my braces were ready to come off. I remember him not charging my dad a penny for taking them off. What a wonderful man. Thus ended my ties to Barium Springs, or so I thought.

I returned in 1967 for homecoming, and one person I remember seeing was Jacob. He told me they were pretty rough on him for a while for running away with me in 1964. Jacob told me that he took a pretty bad beating for running away. There isn't much else I remember about that day, other than remembering how beautiful the campus was. The guys who were there when I ran away in 1964 had already left. I can remember the homecomings we had when I was at Barium in the late fifties and early sixties. So many people came. We would go to church and then have a big lunch under the trees behind one of the cottages. I can't remember the name of the cottage, but I'm sure many of those people who were at Barium during that time can remember. It seemed as though there were enough tables set up to feed an entire army. I know there had to be at least thirty to forty yards of tables there. The one thing I can remember—and remember very well—is what was served for lunch. We always had barbecue, my favorite food. If I remember correctly, we also had homemade ice cream.

I received a call in 1999 or 2000 from a friend of mine who was at Barium with me in the sixties. His name is Gary, and he lives in Florida. He has a daughter who lives in Charlotte, and he told me that he would be heading my way soon. He wanted to know if I would like to ride to Barium. I was all for it. We planned to meet at a restaurant near where his daughter lived. When he got to Charlotte, he gave me a call. We met at the restaurant, had a nice lunch, and headed to Barium. Gary asked me if I would like to visit Mr. Landis while we were at Barium. He said we could stop by the Barium office and find out where he lived. I wasn't crazy about the idea, but I agreed to go visit Mr. Landis with Gary. We stopped by the office and found out that Mr. Landis lived less than half a mile from the Barium campus. We drove over to his house and knocked on the door. When his wife came to the door, we told her who we were, and she invited us in. She took us to the room where Mr. Landis was. He remembered both of us, but he did seem a little cold to me. I don't know if Gary picked up on the coldness or not. What I remember about that room was that there were hundreds of magazines on the floor. I had never seen anything like that in my life. There was not one area of that room that didn't have a magazine on it. Gary told him that when he was in the service, he was an army ranger. I think Mr. Landis was shocked to hear that. He was an ex-marine, and he and Gary made small talk about the service. I just listened.

Finally, I asked Mr. Landis if he remembered some of the things I did at Barium. He said he didn't remember much about that time. I don't know if he didn't remember or if he just didn't want to talk about it. I didn't push the subject because I didn't really want to talk about it either. I shouldn't have brought the subject up. We visited with him for about forty-five minutes and were on our way. That was the last time I ever talked to Mr. Landis. Gary and I headed back to Charlotte. He and

I still talk regularly by phone and e-mail.

In 2010, I went back for homecoming and saw many of my old friends. I had talked to many of them by phone or e-mail to find out who was going to be there. There were plenty of people there that I hadn't seen in forty-five years. What a wonderful time I had reminiscing about old times with all my brothers and sisters. Today, I talk to many of them by phone, e-mail, and Facebook. We will never lose that special bond we have. We were family in the true sense of the word, and that will never change.

The biggest change I see at Barium today is how the whole layout has changed. When I was there as a kid, we had a dairy, orchard, farm, cafeteria, laundry, carpentry shop, and plumbing shop. All of that is now gone. I know that times have changed, and Barium is not Barium Springs Home for Children anymore. Sure, the name is there, but it just isn't the same as it was when I was there as a kid. The farm is no longer there. All the land we worked, tilled, and harvested as children is still there, but all that beautiful rolling land is now nothing but woods. A person going to Barium today for the very first time could never imagine that at one time there was a workable farm there. It is so sad to see what has happened to the land. The same thing can be said about the orchard. All the apple and peach trees are gone. There is nothing there but woods. I, along with the other boys who worked at the orchard, spent many hours pruning and spraying the apple and peach trees, getting them ready to bear fruit. The same thing can be said about the dairy. There are no more pastures where the cows grazed or where we used to sled in the winter. That, too, is nothing but woods. It really hurts to see what has happened to all the land that we as kids used to work with our hands and also play on to our hearts' content. We all know things happen for a reason, but at times I wish I could go back in time and relive the times I was at Barium. The times were good and bad, but mostly good, thanks to my Barium brothers and sisters, who I will never forget. Now I really look forward going to homecoming again more than ever.